PRAISE FO

"*This Radiant Life* strikes a resonant chord with its sparse minimalism. This indexical poetry records private activities, travels, daily living, and details the body's nervous system alongside sudden explosions of brutal events and media frameworks. A capacity for complexity through elliptical building blocks. Violence side by side with train journeys. Collective brutality side by side with personal intimacy or physiological flow. Very few words are hosted on each of these aerated pages. Turning the page in itself confirms the implicit need for breathing space, or for trying to make some sense of it all, while being carried along the currents of one's own time. Everything intermingled. Inescapable as the butterfly effect. Words work like knots of awareness down the rope of lines."

—Caroline Bergvall

"Oscillating between various subatomic particles, spaces, and word matter that make life *life*—i.e. the stuff and messiness of being, the macro and the micro, the chemistry, biology, geology, language of experience/experiment—*This Radiant Life* entreats us to slow down, attend to, and cherish the elemental. In so doing, we will have access to an inexhaustible force for resistance and resilience; we will be able to truly see and be seen by others. Powerfully embodied and chiselled by Chantal Neveu and deftly and intricately translated by Erín Moure, *This Radiant Life* is urgent, alive, and absolutely present."

—Oana Avasilichioaei

"As Chantal Neveu and Erín Moure mine the mono-dimensional sediment of language, they liberate a vocabulary of synaesthetic perception. *This Radiant Life* crushes narrative and reference, not into parts of speech but into illuminated particles, 'words as such.' In this trans-collaboration, words reciprocate the speed and spaces on the perimeter of public sensibility. Gangues of language like 'eye to eye' 'word flow' in the face of the Arab Springs, 'the sound of paper,' 'coffee/ reheated/ on the hob,' 'zig…zag' float by as radiant flecks and syllables on a perceptual horizon. Each turn of the page carries an echo of isolate light, the answer to what happens next."
—Fred Wah

THIS

RADIANT

LIFE

translated by Erín Moure

CHANTAL NEVEU

Book*hug Press
Toronto, 2020 | Literature in Translation Series

FIRST ENGLISH EDITION

Published originally under the title *La vie radieuse* © 2016 by Chantal Neveu and La Peuplade. This edition is published by arrangement with Éditions La Peuplade in conjunction with its duly appointed agent L'Autre agence, Paris, France.

English translation © 2020 by Erín Moure

ALL RIGHTS RESERVED

No part of this publication may be reproduced or transmitted in any form or by any means, electronic or mechanical, including photocopying, recording, or any information storage or retrieval system, without permission in writing from the publisher.

Library and Archives Canada Cataloguing in Publication

Title: This radiant life / Chantal Neveu ; translated by Erín Moure.
Other titles: La vie radieuse. English
Names: Neveu, Chantal, 1964– author. | Moure, Erín, 1955– translator.
Series: Literature in translation series.
Description: First English edition. | Series statement: Literature in translation series | A poem. | Translation of: La vie radieuse.
Identifiers: Canadiana (print) 2020033154X | Canadiana (ebook) 20200331590
ISBN 9781771666336 (softcover) | ISBN 9781771666343 (EPUB)
ISBN 9781771666350 (PDF) | ISBN 9781771666367 (Kindle)
Classification: LCC PS8577.E7597 V5413 2020 | DDC C841/.54—dc23

PRINTED IN CANADA

The production of this book was made possible through the generous assistance of the Canada Council for the Arts and the Ontario Arts Council. Book*hug Press also acknowledges the support of the Government of Canada through the Canada Book Fund and the Government of Ontario through the Ontario Book Publishing Tax Credit and the Ontario Book Fund.

Book*hug Press acknowledges that the land on which it operates is the traditional territory of many nations, including the Mississaugas of the Credit, the Anishnabeg, the Chippewa, the Haudenosaunee and the Wendat peoples. We also recognize the enduring presence of many diverse First Nations, Inuit and Métis peoples and are grateful for the opportunity to meet and work on this territory.

Les mots mêmes.
Words as such.
Paul-Marie Lapointe

Shift the verbal. Utter another language. Invent another speech. Shift writing; write within writing. With no worldly reference other than words. Words as such. Freed from their gangues, from imposed uses, known meanings, accepted paths, from their servitude to thought, which is to say to the "understood" endlessly repeated and sterile.

Paul-Marie Lapointe
"Fragments//Illustrations"

before there's blood there's water

the burning desire to walk

together

on the Mountain

spontaneously

our sexes

separated

called upon

wrists

chosen

our palms

rich

the hours

our throats

on equal footing

the mirror

our embodied plenitude

a frame of trees

the light

it's major

our hearts take form before our hemispheres

so it is with our connection

we have no need to speak

life is long

beautiful

we have a wall

against which

the sky's the same

unique

in living

love

the inside in reverse

the air

a tree

for example

V

a slowness

primordial

attraction

Fe

at the heart

of the Earth

I don't know

before

from where

from which meteorites

haut
up

bas
down

dessous
bottom

dessus*

top

---

* Transl. note: the names of quarks.

we are not alone

we stand

in packs

magnets

twenty-five

Charm, Strange

we vibrate

our letters

the irises

the strings

ten

indivisible

our names

our busts

without hierarchy

photons

intermediaries

in transition

two

three

the immense

canyon

dense and tender

Kr

from the Greek

hidden

He

gas and rare earths

noble

bedrock

the flanks

the branches

the arms

the length of bodies

exposed

nearly inert

framed

we move

everything moves

our gangues

the snow

the clouds

it's a region?

diaphanous

beauty

provisional

our nuggets

the roots

quarks

plates too

a reserve

of negatives

4 x 5

our flavours

electrical charge

the species

source of radiance

of emission

spectra

safe from air

its humidity

Ir

almost absent from Earth's crust

silvery

titanium

the improbable

on the path

in the core

of planets

in pure form or alloy

our poles

desert-like

gold colour

Zr

from the Arabic

from the Persian

the hyacinth

scarab-shaped

of the ancient

Egyptians

fertile

the brilliance

of our eyes

elements

amid known bodies

through

the ground glass

the eyelids

hemoglobin

I recognize

mystery

relation

uninhibited

I no longer fear rupture

corruption

doubled "r"

double

triple

les genres

we are

the others

mediums

clearing

frères & soeurs

the same water

our straits

the tailrace

ahead

in mid-

ford

we are alive

we go

willingly

sensation of common good

word flow

locked or unlocked

there are different speeds

don't run out of breath

don't kill it

there's lots of latitude

things come naturally

just because it's fun

it's different for each person

the detail

du point de vue éthique

eye to eye

with an amplification

see you see me

we give it a try

climatisation

the distance each day

naught

in extremis

physical

regular

constant and irregular

incarnés

much love

at the very least

the time is short

okay

back to concert

magnificent

thanks for the rose

life is transitory

it's a mindset

it's stable

at this point

respiration profonde

it's elementary

the enclosures

a luminousness

you are free

the sky its chemistry

this is the frame

the passage

the demise

it alters things

you see it all

it's all there

the hum

the Sun

ubiquitous

Near

Middle

East

a mass

compact

a human chain

as you can see

des personnes

grazed

by real

bullets

we stand together

against the dictator

we deliver

a will of steel

we persist

it's no time for divisions

for imposing ideologies

eyes bandaged

I sit and sing to myself

fear has left us

we have groundsheets

tarpaulins

light-coloured

bonfires

in the square

assembled

against the police state

dans la rue

knuckles unclenched

index and middle

raised

V

we're alert

at every moment

zigzagzigzagzigzag

Friday of Anger

the sound of tanks

grenades tossed into the crowd

a violent eruption

ionized particles

cloud of plasma

1000 km/h

toward Earth

a new solar cycle

eleven years

phase délicate

impact

on electronic

networks

we can perceive

the aurora borealis

Tahrir

all over Egypt

in every country

such cohesion

miraculous

let's celebrate

victory for dignity

an incredible synergy

the pyramids

weddings

the power of the young

the country fired up

news reports

SMS

militia positions

on Twitter

we saved lives

people didn't back off even a centimetre

we are strong

we can ask ourselves

what role the army will play

numbers reassure us

khamsin kamsin chamsin

fifty days in springtime

windstorms

sands

dark orange

burning

150 km/h

from the deserts of Egypt right to Israel

millions of citizens

ever ready

to protest

march

defend

write

a constitution

partial media blackout in China

suddenly

the birds

Cardinalis cardinalis

it's unspeakable

the water table gushes oil

we can be killed

a law

condemns to death all who resist him

no to the sequestering of revolutions

Mars

even closer

tonight

water blood-jasmine on the hands

cupped in the palms

between the fingers

chaos on the ground

the radicals our prisms our moods

our armaments our currency

our tongues

witnesses

in the arena

poetry

a correlation

a regime

coalescence

how close are the bodies?

there's something more

in the material

the pulses

cinnabar

miasmas

petal

metal

fuchsia

pleated

waters the waters the waters

lakes continents mountains and forests

resin

sound of paper

what I deduce

outside the text

a density a sum is transformed

infra

simultaneously

subjugations prescriptions

geometries pages

plans

otherwise

fitting

the moon by day translucent

without exotic matter

in the field

four cocks

plus a hen

right to the talus

the quality

of loose

earth

plants raspberries

sage

garlic

rosemary

potatoes

in quantity

under the leaves

the well

a pump

septic system

points of reference

on the land survey

an X

to the west of the west the east

is a quality a direction?

crisp October air

the apples

windfallen

a degree of reality

orientation

wool

the coffee

reheated

on the hob

oxblood

the barn

a needle

of hawthorn

tip

embedded

right calf

gathering branches

dead

wood

still green

take a few sips

pondering bone-dry

leather-hard

select trees select boards

length of spruce

weight-bearing timbers

heart to the outside

as ever

centre marked

chalk line

marges de manœuvre

three rooms

the study

the oven

the tower

sawdust

the stove

the staircase

the question of doors

of landings

squared out

practical

steps angled

two or three

the angle of rise

flight

seventeen step-heights

main axis ascending

incline

a house

a building

so that it is

soft

the lilac

late-bloom

solstice daisies peonies

facades rising over polyhedrons

walls smooth silvery

the wind

the effect on speed

hygiene of immanence

we tend to

a goat

the donkey

their hooves

trimmed

the eggs

sweet

corn

from west to east here

the hill

the path

the generations

lambswool held by furring strips

the river beneath

the plain

meeting point

in America

the heat wave

to sleep

open air

is like sleeping sans floor

outside

on one's back

between breaths in and out

to suspend

to prolong breath

the pelvic channel

astride

likewise

skin against skin

to embrace

deep nature

Amerindian

Innu

an identical humanity

walking

discerning

the rings

of Saturn

telescopic

indigenous

we relinquish

we turn

is it an idyll?

the soil matters to us

combat area

a square in a square

we dissociate hostilities

focal points of aggressivity

heels light

weight distributed

on the soles of the feet

blinking

magenta

in a fraction of a second

a détente

an opening

the entry

it's the moment

harmony is

or isn't

to each attack

a precise

reaction

simultaneous

a legitimate

defence

gestural

immediate

proportionate

reversible

a channel

energy

cardinal

kinetic

pivots sideslips facing

eyelids blades

fall

we too

exemplary

conveyors

imperfection and elegance

in various moves

our art our steps

resonance of rhythmic

indices

and sympathetic systems

meridians

circular sweeps and other cardiac

graph lines

our tunics

haptic

markers

soot

of pine

needles

sepia

infrangible bodies

outside laws

the words

hinges

hinge pins

our plasticity

stomachs and brains

pelvic birds not visible

paintbrushes

the gravity between the hips

our base

with the air

we train

for suppleness

suchness

speed

with taut amplitude

minima maxima

under the rotation

of propellers

the sound

heli-co-

pters poli-ce

on the plateau

agora

long sticks short sticks

we hurl forward

in all directions

all shapes and sizes

men and women

dancing bodies

all ages

we enter

the situation

and in keeping with

the best of forms

we create

dozens

thousands

dozens of thousands of techniques

to absorb

to bend to deviate

fists and vectors

to unbalance

to immobilize

in placing ourselves

remobilizing

with resources energies

the North

we ready ourselves

to attend practise anticipate hone

the void

space

diamondine

carbonic

bare-handed

here is your heart

emperor

see it

can you hear it?

attuned to values

now

it vibrates

firepower

electromagnetic in its field

five thousand times stronger than the brain

it's amazing

you can forget who you are

you can simply be

finally

totally

be

power generating power

centred

with

the rest

of the stars

extinguished

exoplanets

provisional agglomerates

similar

our liquids

pupils

lasers

our channels

are they tubes?

I marvel

is this life?

radiant

electricity

pips of silica

our seed germ

carbon

their liaisons

reflections

is this light?

what we form

together

mountain

rock seated

shadows

slopes

concordant profiles

enigma of our sediments

pulsations

ignorance organic anatomic

subatomic

nano

we turn around

into

a milieu

negligible variance

dissolution of controversies

we all feel

alive and living

fine

dispossessed

disentangled

I want to say delivered

neither subject

nor object

in the magma

feu

someone has died

a person an animal

mourning and rebirth

initiations

lemmas

to augment the real

with fire

a thing ancient

and the Sun

still

matrix

in being

our bones

pulsions

fascias

sulphur

flash

your face is returning my mother tells me

vast night

above the Atlantic

les astres

so close

through the porthole glass

constellations without name

entanglement of scales

Zaventem

the air

on the runway

inversed convection

locate black taxis into Brussels

Bruxelles

"x"

double "s"

a fluid topology

camera intercom stairwell

muffled vestibule

jet lag

new slowness

climb upstairs

on the second floor a patio

a solarium

into the atmosphere

Delvaux putty-white ash-grey

rosemary bushes colour of North Sea

afterglow

Ostend

the sound this makes

to the southwest

GPS

Vollezele

a direct

diagonal

Chaussée de Ninove

perpendicular

50 km/h

prosaic road syntax

alert to speed cameras

market-garden zone

architectonics of brick

pale or brown

the farms

deserted primitive Flemish paintings

Hellebosch

tall beechwoods

laden with suitcases books

questions

adjacent tongues

we shed it all

facing

the garden

a clearing

upstairs

long hallway

high humidity

dark green ambience mirror

estate surrounding

busts doors

behind which an upright piano

an alcove

tiny

under narrow-slit window

a bed

small

clearly not meant to splay out on

easygoing

reorient the 80 centimetres

into a sky bed

austerity in plenitude

somatic disappointment in *vita nova*

re-

ascetic

skeleton in a pareo

so as to practise

is this the dao?

rest sacrum and lymph

nap in daylight

to recalibrate time zones

risen then

around a table

happy connivances

immediate

circumstantial

welcome

laugh

smile

drinking wine

tea

early morning a bad dream

a quill aside the heart

hand of the ex-spouse holding the arm

a dare

an amusement a threat or a gentleness

liberation

life lucid or elucidated

a click

to not be dead

not about to die either

not now

now

re-

live

is this a reviving?

across from

bathroom

office

under miniature

Vermeer

window

photons slant from on high

across the writing desk

inset leather moons

that which

there to keep still

there to bring forth

there

to oxygenate

shoulder girdle

bony triad

humerus radius ulna

the innervation

from the pubis

to the pinna of the ear

floor

mature

to breathe

to secrete

from deep down

in the interval

thoracic

cavity

expanded

vacant

is it generating?

that which

syntagms in the making

to say to not say

to babble

to blow out

to smelt down

the logos

to write to not write

this life

radiant

idyll

brief form

prolonged

including

le hors-champ

contingencies

even

adversity

in the mode of a murmur

Cage's question

what is harmony?

to love

to walk

to drive

to love

bamboo

thighs

cyclists

the dairy

cows

to go off

to Ghent

to face

the Altarpiece

the van Eycks

the Adoration

of the Lamb

Mystic

the gathering of women

palm fronds

Eve

Adam

foot raised

on the way back

to see again

the lambs

graze

in Pajottenland

is it birth?

singing

at the wheel

take a walk

on the wild side

all is economy

architecture

culture agriculture contiguous

one inside the other

domesticity and linguistics

nothing is anecdotal

the mutations

invisible

discrete

radiations

possessions

dispossessions

the alternation

rapture reversed into rapture

loss into delight

the difference between committed and obliged

that which is

that which might be—or not

potentia

attention

lexicon

poésie

verticale

frugal

lush

peaceable

pacifying

vita activa

it's in the voice

syllables rebound

stamina

maieutics

put into play

into world

practices

routes

to extend ourselves

to keep apprehending

to comprehend

to come to know

to translate

to emerge

above the willow

mass more pale

in the park

propulsion beneath a balloon

aerial sequence

right to the roof ridge

concave furrow

on each side

of the spinal column

gutter

under the cornice

below near the roses

hedgerows

disconcerting

cosmetic landscape

a solitary hare

between dog and wolf

a rider

falls

dazed

nonplussed

yes

that's it

non plus

to transform perplexity

the ration

what no longer is

what had been rationalized

into gaiety

that's what connects us

the day the dawn

after rain showers

exquisite sensation

the aureoles over the orchard

dahlias nasturtiums fennel squashes

in the pasture

the old horse tears the grass

with his huge mouth

chews

swallows

defecates

outside the paddock

beets

tall stalks of corn

vis-à-vis

we're the same

noon

to open the window

the dog

friend

arrives

to share bread gouda

daily egg yolk

the world news

wars

decapitations

explosions

elections

Ebola

Nobel

succulents

sempervivum

we live together

monsters

eros

adorable

mean

what do you mean?

are we amiable

sufficiently loving

on the landing

monstera

large palms

in fingers

same plant in the studio in Montreal

duos dyads binomes

hands dealt us

is this autonomy?

infinity's horizontal eight between the hips

behind the willow

a tall hedge

shattered

by lightning

its long branches like so many limbs

that had not foreseen

their fall

we don't desist in our mutualities

it's good to be giving

we don't belong to each other

we belong to the whole

specimens

beyond possession

soma & germen

we move

from source to source

in the interstices

we breathe

fresh energies

phrenic centres

symbiosis

pneuma

from our lips

bubbles

floating

suspended

transparent

radiant

seven

globes

polymers

solar

plexus

amid our chests

buds

dense horde

chlorophyll

bedded in white silica

our hearts

mixed gases

O=C=O

light

photo

synthesizing

in vivo

before our eyes

in so many loggias

7.7 billion

philia

opera

of our breathing

millimetric

seedlings

wide range

pH

balanced

linked

our senses silent

in exchanging

on the spot

we change

explicitly

vitae data capta

exo eso abolished

fair growth

seeds crucifers sprigs leaves

radish brassica yukina

amaranth mizuna arugula

Abyssinian

mustard

aligned with the equinoxes

we go on

                          allons

collaborating

                          collaborant

co-op & monitoring

                          co-op & monitoring

spring banquet

                          banquet de printemps

primavera

                          primavera

we intermingle

                          nous nous mélangeons

we eat

                          mangeons

grateful

                          reconnaissants

RADIANCE: A POSTFACE

1

Translating Chantal Neveu is more than a work with and through words and words' proximity; it is also a spatialization that is rhythmic. By this I mean that it is an attention to space, and to breath marked in space,* and to the human eye's capture of words in space. To the cadence that is produced by unfurling syllables, even before these are words charged with semantic value.

La vie radieuse, Neveu's fifth full collection of poetry, not only uses words, space, and adjacency, it deploys and constellates lexicons that are scientific, yet also *somatic, psychic, pneumic*—as in ancient Greek and Hebrew and Chinese philosophies of balanced life. Her lexicons are those of the chemical constituents of the body and of the planet, the lexicons of practices of bodies and the movements of bodies: from Aikido to the world of quarks. In incredibly compact poems, Neveu uses word, sound, spacing, rhythm to examine bodily relations to space, history, environment, climate. To political events and to our desires. Which is to say: to war, genocide, rebirth, scenes, environmental risk, mutuality, and loss. Her "body" here is incarnated as "feminine," and our view of philosophical and plastic gestures is given us through a woman's body (here read this word in its largest sense, not as essential gender), but also a beckoning to *world* (the constructed dimension) and to earth (the elements, and not just the gold but the gangue).

---

* For Chantal Neveu, the blank page, and the interval between words, is like the interval between inspiration and expiration of breath.

In *This Radiant Life*, Neveu metabolizes these lexicons and practices. Words ricochet, firstly, not off each other but off space itself: the conjunction, energy, and absence that is the blank page. Words are rhythmic, as such, as they are placed on that page, even before they meet up with one another. A second major pulsation is the turning of the page: the words move into a lateral extension with the turning of the page—an act performed by the reader.

Her words radiate light, sound, movement, breath from the depth of the solar plexus. There are echoes of Spinoza and Spinozan bodily capacities, and of Moshe Feldenkrais (*The Potent Self*), Mabel Elsworth Todd (*The Thinking Body*), Chuang Tzu, Pascal Quignard, psychoanalyst/hypnotherapist François Roustang, alongside ripples of Dante's *Vita Nova* and of the *vita activa* of Hannah Arendt. Theocritus is present ("is it an idyll?"), and Sappho (see Anne Carson's versions in *If Not Winter*). The moral philosophy of Ruwen Ogien is a reference, the gravity of Ushio Amagatsu, and the historical dictionary of Alain Rey (*Le Robert*). All of these influences, as Neveu says herself, are *metabolized* in a poetic practice of space, sound, syllable where resonance is key.

None of this is surprising. Neveu is both poet and artist, trained in cinema and having worked as a researcher in contemporary art and architecture milieux before she decided to devote her research, creation, and performance practice to poetry. She writes alongside visual artists as well, such as Ana Rewakowicz and Andréanne Michon, who are present in *This Radiant Life*. Neveu's sense of the book and what it makes possible is a "plastic" sense, and here "plastic" does not refer to polymers and their encrustations, but to malleability and the motions that malleability enacts and permits. *Plasticité* is a word very current and useful in French that survives mostly as a suffix in English: thermoplastic, thromboplastic, neoplastic, etc., although we do speak of the plasticity of the brain. In that word lies the movement that is creation. The life that is radiant in creation, despite the terrible obstacles, the adversities. Further, reading itself is plastic, kinesthetic: we turn pages, we move our eyes, and these movements and turnings help construct our reception of what we read.

In being aware of movement in all the senses, in all directions, Neveu's minimalism allows her to practise a "reversability" of words and syntagms, of actions, of segments: inviting an experience of their polysemy. The work is not driven by a subjectivity that legislates, moralizes, or declares, but by an ethics of movement in response to situations.

2

My first intention, in proposing to translate *La vie radieuse*, was to enjoy the chance to work with Chantal Neveu in physical space and in real time. I was to bring my first draft of the work—with its attention to space, sound, rhythm, etymology, echo—into the physical space of a studio where we could work together on the revision as two embodied beings, francophone poet and polyphone anglo translator, in space that could act on us somatically to modulate the words, the spatialization, through allowing the living presence of voice, timbre, gesture, accent, echo.

At the moment the first draft was complete at the end of May 2019, the political and social terrain on which the book was founded in 2010–15 had changed, altered, and not in any good sense: wars, economic collapses, genocides, environmental disaster were ever closer to us. Perhaps, we postulated, some of this altered terrain would enter in an unpredictable way into the translated book in its new language, its new ambience. My idea at the time was to encourage Neveu to bring in new words, coalects, turns, in response to what she had written several years earlier; I would monitor her response to her own words and see how time had altered them, had reactivated their plasticity in the reintroduction into new spaces, and a new tongue. And perhaps, as a result, we would gather something new into the English work as well. It was a process intended to take translation beyond the mere seeking of "equivalents," in order to attend as well to the spaces into which the new work would arrive, attend to the new ears. *This Radiant Life*, after all, keeps on beaming outward to its public, its new publics, its readers.

In the end, illness cut short that initial plan. Grave physical illness, weeks in ICU: a battle for life. And then a calamitous late spring of floods (Neveu's line "waters the waters the waters" was prescient), as Lake Ontario soaked into Gibraltar Point on Toronto Island and forced the closure of the residency program at Artscape, where I'd reserved the studio and living space for the revision process.

Cut loose then from the plan, and detained in Montreal, the work was still in progress, even though nothing was being actively revised. As the poet recovered her energies and capacities, the radiance of life itself was my companion, and hers. We walked and talked. We drank coffee. We watched the lilac blossoms fall in a shady courtyard in the east of Montreal. We discovered the joy of benches. We ignored the book and the translation.

Or we seemed to ignore it: for in fact we were entering into it more fully, each of us in our own way changed by the passage of months in each of our lives. The rhythms and lexicon of the work came quickly to us, and Chantal recounted to me, as we sat together to review the translation late in the year, the origins of some lexicon, the exact coloration of a word or movement, the images of dark and light that were her influences, and I was able to find new ways to revise the translation. Chantal Neveu is so encouraging, so pleased: she doesn't expect that her work will be duplicated by the translation, but knows that it is a new work, out of the old work, that is finding its way into the world, bringing us with it, her as author, and me as translator.

As translator, I'll say that the challenges of a minimalist text are many, as each word in the original calls on aspects of its own register and confection that are silent in its own culture, embedded in it, unspoken. Words are not just articulated noise! In bringing the work into a new culture and set of sounds, I had not only to create new sounds, words, relations, to give the poems in English a similar momentum, I also had to take care that the silences in English to which my word choices beckoned were also articulate silences, articulate spacings, and contributed to the text. I had to translate reverberations and blank spaces. They are critical: they are what link the words and allow them to flow. Fortunately, Chantal generously made herself available for working, and with her elaborate record-keeping of her collaborative work with visual artists and her philosophical readings, she was able to dig out and show me images, references, vocabularies that allowed me to find words that could articulate but also sculpt the silences of the work in its new English clothes.

As we worked together in December 2019 and January 2020, pre-pandemic, to create the final version, we realized that the book resonates politically in 2020 just as intently as it did in 2016, and has no need of additions. The turmoil of the drive for freedom of peoples that marked the Arab Springs and is so vivid in the political field of references in *La vie radieuse*, echoes in *This Radiant Life* in the tensions still ongoing in the Middle East, and where we live in Canada, for East now is forever imbricated in West, changing it, and us. As readers, as persons. We, readers of Chantal Neveu: we hope, for the world's sake, for an increase in all our lives of the mutualities—and of the reversabilities, the polysemy and ethical dwelling—that *This Radiant Life* so generously intends and extends to us. Our health as humans, thinkers, progenitors, co-creators, sharers—before, in, and post-pandemic—depends on this.

Erín Moure
Montreal, January and August 2020

ACKNOWLEDGEMENTS

The epigraph from Paul-Marie Lapointe on page vii is from "Fragments//Illustrations" in *L'espace de vivre : poèmes 1968–2002*. (Montreal, Hexagone, 2004, page 613, translation here by E.M.)

The poet thanks her translators and editors, and the artists with whom she has collaborated. English variations of several texts from *La vie radieuse* have appeared:

- at Galerie Armatta (Montréal) and on the website of photographer Andréanne Michon in resonance with her series *Charm, Strange*, 2011 (tr. Angela Carr);
- *The Capilano Review* 3.20, spring 2013 (tr. Angela Carr);
- *Imperceptibly and Slowly Opening*, ed. Caroline Picard. Chicago: Green Lantern Press, 2016, in resonance with the installation LSS *(Life Support System)* by artist Ana Rewakowicz (tr. Nathanaël);
- *Columba* 3, spring 2020, www.columbapoetry.com (tr. Erín Moure).

The translator thanks Chantal Neveu for her intense engagement in the process of translation and revision, and thanks Oana Avasilichioaei, Caroline Bergvall, and Fred Wah for their friendship in poetry, and for their generous words that hail and welcome Chantal's work.

CHANTAL NEVEU is the author of five books of poetry: *La vie radieuse*; *coït*; *mentale* (all La Peuplade); *Une spectaculaire influence* (l'Hexagone); and *èdres* (É=É), and has created numerous interdisciplinary literary works, produced and presented in Canada and abroad. She has work in many magazines and anthologies: *Cyclages/Grupmuv* (École des arts visuels et médiatiques/UQAM), *Espaces de savoir* (Université Laval), and *Laboratoire parcellaire* (OBORO/La Peuplade), and has held residencies at Maison de la poésie de Nantes (France), Passa Porta and Villa Hellebosch (Belgium), and Villa Waldberta (Germany). Book*hug has published two previous books by Neveu: *Coït* (tr. Angela Carr) and *A Spectacular Influence* (tr. Nathanaël).

ERÍN MOURE has published over forty books: poetry, essays, memoir, and translations and co-translations from French, Spanish, Galician, Portuguese, Portunhol, and Ukrainian. Recent translations: *In Leaf* by Rosalía de Castro (Zat-So Productions, 2019), *The Uplands: Book of the Courel and other poems* by Uxío Novoneyra (Veliz Books, 2020), and *Sleepless Nights Under Capitalism* by Juan Gelman (Eulalia Books, 2020). Moure holds two honorary doctorates from universities in Canada and Spain, was 2017 Creative Fellow at Harvard's Woodberry Poetry Room, and 2019 International Translator in Residence at Queen's College, Oxford. In process: Chus Pato's *The Face of the Quartzes* and Andrés Ajens's *So-Lair Storm*.

Colophon

Manufactured as the first English edition of
This Radiant Life
in the fall of 2020 by Book*hug Press

Copy-edited by Stuart Ross
Type + design by Michel Vrana

bookhugpress.ca